NATIVE ANIMALS of HAWAI'I Coloring Book

Written and Illustrated
by
Patrick Ching

Bess Press, Inc.
P.O. Box 22388
Honolulu, HI 96822

NATIVE ANIMALS OF HAWAI'I is a coloring book designed to familiarize you with the special animals of Hawai'i. All of the animals in this book are "Native" to Hawai'i; that means they arrived in the islands *without* the help of man.

On the upper left hand corner of each information sheet is the word "endemic," "migratory," or "indigenous." The word "endemic" refers to animals that exist only in Hawai'i, while the word "indigenous" refers to native animals that live in Hawai'i as well as in other parts of the world.

If the word "threatened" or "endangered" appears on the upper right corner of the information page, it is to indicate the survival status of the animal as it is classified by the Federal Government. (*A large percent of the "threatened" or "endangered" species in the USA exists in Hawai'i.)

COLORING: Color Crayons or Colored Pencils are recommended for coloring this book. For accurate coloring, look at the small pictures on the back of this book and use them as a guide.

HAWAIIAN HONEYCREEPER
('I'iwi)

The brilliantly colored 'I'iwi inhabit the upper forests of Hawai'i, Maui and Kaua'i. They are very rare on O'ahu and Moloka'i.

A favorite food of these birds is the nectar from the *lehua* blossom of the native *'Ōhi'a* tree.

The 'I'iwi is one of over forty species of Hawaiian honeycreeper that are believed to have evolved from a common ancestral species that arrived in Hawai'i millions of years ago.

The bright red feathers of the 'I'iwi were used by the ancient Hawaiians to make helmets, capes, and other feathered articles.

PACIFIC GREEN SEA TURTLE
(Honu)

The Pacific Green Sea Turtle can be found in waters throughout the Pacific. The main breeding grounds for these turtles are on the remote islands of the northwest Hawaiian chain.

Young Green Sea Turtles may eat seaweed as well as tiny marine animals. Adult Green Sea Turtles feed almost entirely on seaweed and algae.

The Green Sea Turtle did not get its name from the color of its shell, which is more brown than green, but instead was named for the color of its flesh and body fluids which are green as a result of its diet of seaweed. (*Today it is illegal to capture or kill sea turtles or their eggs).

HAWAIIAN LAND SNAIL
(Pūpū-kani-oe)

Hawaiian Land Snails can be seen crawling about on native plants in the upper rain forests on most of the main Hawaiian Islands.

Hawaiian Land Snails, eat fungi and algae off the leaves of native plants (much like tiny vacuum cleaners.)

There are over one thousand species of native land snails in Hawai'i; many of them are threatened with extinction.Two reasons for this are loss of habitat and predation by introduced animals such as rats and cannibal snails.

PARROT FISH
(Uhu)

Parrot Fish are common throughout tropical oceans. They live in relatively shallow reef areas around all the Hawaiian Islands.

Parrot Fish eat seaweed that grows on coral reefs. They get their name because of their parrot-like beaks which they use to bite off chunks of coral from the reef. The coral turns to sand as it passes through their bodies while the algae that was growing on the coral is digested by the fish.

HAWAIIAN HAWK
('Io)

On the island of Hawai'i, hawks can sometimes be seen soaring in circles high above the ground or perched atop a tree in search of prey.

Their meals consist of rodents, insects, stream animals and other birds.

The Hawaiian Hawk and Hawaiian Short-Eared Owl (Pueo) are the only native birds of prey living in Hawai'i today. Fossil remains tell us that a sea-eagle and other native species of hawk and owl previously existed.

HAWAIIAN MONK SEAL
('Īlio-holo-i-kauaua)

Hawaiian Monk Seals inhabit the tiny islands and atolls located northwest of Kaua'i.

A monk seal's diet consists of fish, octopus and other marine animals.

Mother monk seals give birth to a single jet-black pup. The pup feeds on its mother's milk for about five weeks. During this time the mother monk seal does not eat and is always by her pup's side. One day the mother monk seal will leave her pup and it must learn to catch food for itself.

KAMEHAMEHA BUTTERFLY
(Pulelehua)

The Kamehameha Butterfly can be seen fluttering about Hawaiian forests on most of the main Islands.

The favorite food of the Kamehameha caterpillar is the native *mamaki* plant. Adult butterflies feast on the sap that seeps out of certain trees such as the native *koa* tree (not shown).

The Kamehameha Butterfly is one of only two butterflies that are native to Hawai'i. (However, there are many species of native Hawaiian moths.)

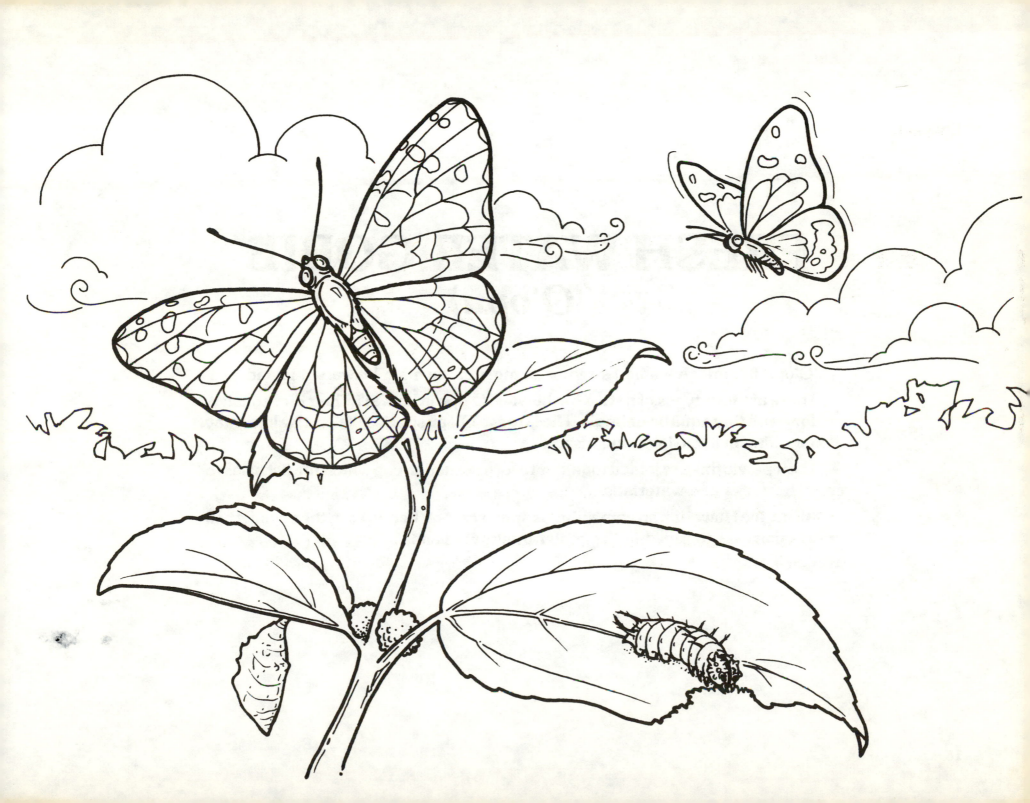

FRESH WATER GOBIE
('O'opu)

'O'opu inhabit rivers and streams of most of the main Hawaiian Islands.

There are four types of native freshwater 'O'opu in Hawai'i. Their diet consists of algae and tiny aquatic animals. The largest 'O'opu species, 'O'opu Nakea, may also eat tiny fish, shrimp, and insects.

Their pelvic fins are joined together to form a suction cup which the fish uses to crawl up rocks and waterfalls.

All native Hawaiian stream animals spend part of their lives in the ocean, then crawl upstream to breed in the cooler mountain ponds.

GREAT FRIGATE BIRD
('Iwa)

Most of the Great Frigate Birds in Hawai'i nest in colonies on the Northwest Hawaiian Islands. There are also a few colonies on or near the main islands. These birds can sometimes be seen soaring high in circles above coastal areas and even venture inland.

The 'Iwa gets its name from its habit of stealing fish from other birds. In Hawaiian, the word *'Iwa* means "thief." Though they are capable of catching fish for themselves, 'Iwa birds will often harass other seabirds into giving up their catch.

During mating season, male Frigate Birds attract females by blowing up their large, red throat pouches.

Ancient navigators watched the flight of the 'Iwa to help them find the direction of land.

HAWAIIAN HOARY BAT
('Ōpe'ape'a)

The native Hawaiian Bat is most common on the islands of Hawai'i and Kaua'i where it spends most of the day hanging out in trees alone or in pairs.

Hawaiian Hoary Bats can be seen fluttering about at dusk in search of insects.

Bats use radar to find food and make their way through the night. By sending out high pitched screams that bounce off objects, the bats can determine the distance of the objects.

HAWAIIAN STILT
(Ae'o)

Hawaiian Stilts can be found in the lower wetland areas of the main Hawaiian Islands.

Their diet consists of fishes, worms, snails, tiny crabs and insects.

Wetland habitats of the Hawaiian Stilt and other native waterbirds are rapidly being filled in and developed. Because of this, most of Hawai'i's wetland birds are in danger of becoming extinct.

OCTOPUS
(He'e)

Octopi inhabit the reefs and tidepools around all Hawaiian Islands.

Octopi feed on shellfish and mollusks. One of their favorite foods is the *leho* or cowry.

The Hawaiians believed that when the sugarcane flowered, the octopus was abundant. They would make special lures for the octopus using the empty shells of the cowry attached to a hook and line. When the octopus wrapped itself around the empty cowry shell, the line was pulled in and the octopus was captured.

PACIFIC GOLDEN-PLOVER
(Kolea)

In August and September the Pacific Golden-Plover arrives in Hawai'i. They come from Arctic breeding grounds where they have spent the summer. These plovers spend their winter months in Hawai'i and other Pacific islands. When April and May come around, the kolea will migrate once again to their arctic nesting grounds.

The Kolea prefer open fields of grass to hunt for insects and snails. They are very territorial and usually return to the same area each year.

The Kolea was often described in Hawaiian legend as a messenger or informer.

SHARK
(Manō)

Many kinds of sharks inhabit the waters around all the Hawaiian Islands.

All sharks eat animals though only a few types are known to attack humans.

In Hawai'i shark skins were used to make drums and shark teeth were used to make cutting tools and weapons. Many Hawaiians worshiped sharks as family guardians or 'aumākua.

HAWAIIAN GOOSE
(Nēnē)

The Nēnē, Hawai'i's state bird, can now be found on the volcanic slopes of Mauna Kea and Hualalai on the island of Hawai'i, and in Haleakalā crater on Maui.

Unlike other kinds of geese, which live near the water, the Nēnē has adapted to living on volcanic slopes with scattered vegetation.

The Nēnē's diet includes seeds, grasses and fruits. The native 'Ōhelo berry is among its favorite foods.

In the late 1950's the Nēnē population was nearly extinct. Through the efforts of a state captive breeding program, the Nēnē's numbers increased and hundreds of birds were reintroduced into the wild.

BOOKS TO READ

Ching, Patrick, *Exotic Animals in Hawai'i Coloring Book*. Honolulu: The Bess Press, 1988.

Shallenberger, Robert J., ed. *Hawaii's Birds*. Honolulu: Hawaii Audobon Society, 1981.

Balazs, George H. *Hawaii's Seabirds, Turtles, and Seals*. Honolulu: World Wide Distributors, Ltd., 1976.

van Riper, Sandra G. and Charles van Riper III, *A Field Guide to the Mammals* in Hawaii. Honolulu: The Oriental Publishing Company, 1982.

Patrick Ching '87

ABOUT THE AUTHOR

Born and raised in Hawai'i, Patrick Ching possesses a deep-rooted love for the islands which is portrayed in his artwork and writings. His enthusiasm for wildlife, art and Hawaiiana is the driving force behind his work. He spends a good deal of time "in the field" working with and observing Hawai'i's animals in their natural environments. Patrick devotes much of his energy toward educating the public about Hawaiian wildlife through slideshow productions, guided nature hikes, and multi-media artwork.

ACKNOWLEDGEMENTS

A special *Mahalo* goes out to the people and organizations who contributed their time and knowledge toward producting this book: Sheila Conant, Bruce Eilerts, John Ford, William G. Gillmartin, Thane Pratt, Robert Pyle, Jack Randal, Lokomaika'iokalani Snakenberg, the Bishop Museum, the Hawaii Audobon Society, Ho'omaluhia Botanic Garden, the National Fish and Wildlife Service, the National Marine Fisheries Service, and the State Department of Land and Natural Resources.